THE GREY ALBUM

[POEMS]

Curtis L. Crisler

THE GREY ALBUM

Curtis L. Crisler

STEEL TOE BOOKS BOWLING GREEN, KENTUCKY

STEEL TOE BOOKS
Western Kentucky University
Department of English
1906 College Heights Blvd. #11086
Bowling Green, Kent. 42101-1086

BOOK DESIGNED BY THOM CARAWAY

Steel Toe Books is affiliated with Western Kentucky University

TABLE OF CONTENTS

Grey Hot Tracks

The Grey Singles

Living in the Grey Matter Cento

Dedicated to my rogue, Prince.

"Life isn't black and white. It's a million gray areas, don't you find?"

    —Ridley Scott

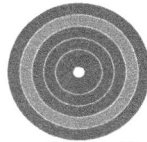

Grey Hot Tracks

LIVING IN GREY MATTERS (A PATTERN)

i.

I am breathing in the day's anaphoras about unarmed boys called
    vultures with busted wings. I am not carrying them
from point A to point B. I am not depleting their air waves, (re)dacting them
    out. I am not calling them nonbeings. They are dying on video,

        before us, giving up the last holy word. I am marked with
an Ida B. welling, a James Cameron keloid memory, or the two-faced science
    of drapetomania. We watch drama, how we commingle with our air,
        but still, visualize one losing his breath. I hate being

a body limped into nonbreathing or the last funneled breath taking on
    a match, no fire to name. So question the above. *How many breaths*
        does it take to own a full life? What does the last gasp
of one person freed into the sinuses of the living taste like—a backwash (re)flux

    wafting, rattling in the living's throats? When one is (re)adjusted,
        who does one call to subdue the (re)adjuster? The people with
badges, (re)adjusting in broad daylight? Oh, there's good badges, (re)adjustees
    who'll fight (re)adjusters. But in the grey coals we all look alike.

    We all add more heat, more sparks and spikes, more dotting
infinite I's, more punctuating news events for how to puncture what's relevant.
    So, question...what is relevant in jotting down our daily injuries on
        sticky notes? When shall our eyes witness, "my breath's

your breath and our breaths are holding cells to life?" When shall we see
    choking a soul out of one ashen body only (re)leases that soul
        back into every living thing.

ii.

I am writing t h r o u g h cloudy hallucinations—b r o k e n
    words s c a t t e r i n g on lined expectations. My words have
turned i t c h y , become anxious for a cypher's punctuation,
    for a phlebotomist of capitalization o v e r the status q u o

of capitalizing. I am breathing in

        the s l a s h i n g of my T's, the nondotting of my I's
            like it's a -10 degrees below-air c o n f i s c a t i n g
    my b r e a t h , like I'm d o w n h i l l i n g , tubeless.
                I'm c r a s h i n g into a sentence,
                    a line, a paragraph, a s t a n z a
                moving from its knees to its feet...

BORN INTO CHAOS

Three years and a day after Norma Jeane Mortenson overdosed into
    her great sleep, I was born

I was born later in the year el-Hajj Malik el-Shabazz's body ate bullets

I was born before Martin's words slid across his moustache, off Lorraine's ledge
    I was about three

I was born before the operatic-Mafioso erasing of Robert Kennedy
    I was three and some change

Fill in time with the Age of Aquarius

Fill in space with us landing on dark side of moon

Fill in the ~~blanks~~ hypotheticals with Woodstock, Mayor Hatcher, Vietnam

Smell the white and black clouds, puffing—
    the lime stench of the city losing its strength

Here, I was placed, like a matchbox child
    with a face of soot and lungs on fire

Here, my mother was born,
    with a face of soot and lungs of fire

Here we live, in the City of Steel,
    slowly oxidizing into its burgundy

MARROW

Looking at gathered chicken bones
    a manmade beaver dam on a plate   takes me

back to my mutt   Lady   shepherd mixed with
    another soup in doggy DNA   How apropos

even for humans   She would devour these bones
    mixed with her crunchy dog dinner   I scrape

the scraps into the garbage   thinking *I eat chicken*
    when dogs today eat shrimp   filet mignon   rice

and vegetables   not table scraps   How heavy that
    word "change"   Were we lucky no bones ever

got stuck in her throat?   Or did evolution change
    the way dogs take things in   with all this hybrid-

mixing?   Were my parents lucky   as well   no bones
    of catfish   of buffalo   got stuck in my throat?

What are the wolf   the coyote   the wild dog   and stray
    doing incorrectly when eating boney things?

I place greasy plate under hot sink water   wash
    away residue of centrical thoughts   When a boy

we took in hairy wet strays   As a man   the streets
    are strayless   The bones in garbage   singing

SINGING HER AUGUSTA SAVAGE MODE

—for photo "Theresa 2003" by Dawoud Bey

The multi-colored blues you wear sing their Chi-town infamy. Your eyes say things. There is an every-day teenager battling the throes of adulthood with how it was to be six and in love with seeing tomorrow. Things steppin' like those Saturday-night-steppers from your fifteen-year old heart. You are twenty-six now, and I wonder what blues you wear this Friday. I wonder if the South Shore took you to woman-hood too fast, or did the train break down, and you had to bus it into the matriarchal sundress of rhythm that beats underneath your eyes. They draw us to you, Chi-town's dark Mona Lisa. Like everyone who sat in that wooden chair, before and after you, they have worn dreams like sweaters that resist cold. I once sat in the same moment too, but I could never be the girl with a dark thick nose and thick lips and African eyes that morphed into Mondays and next weeks. I could never be the woman that you are now, moving into new chapters of gardening, growing like Fauna's tomorrows. I could never be the Augusta wind you know, blowing against the bending flowers, how to replicate through the maneuvers of your hands, those children who will sit in wooden chairs and wonder their worth. Theresa, I am saying your name to bring you back from one existence to the now, and you are here, watching over us through the magic of art. Theresa, the etymology of you is just beginning, but has been forever. I am in your eyes, looking back at all children—your Chi-town, your wooden chairs, your Augusta Savageness.

THE BURNING DANCE LESSON

—for Tata

In my girlfriend's dorm room,
    in Bloomington,
        eating pizza, all kissy

face before the breaking news
    ...MANDELA...IS...FREE...
        We whoop whoop and all

electric. We kiss for freedom. Pizza breath—
    black and young and renaissancing
        on an African man

scraping off 27 years of dust
    like it was cleaning out
        the lint in his pocket—

knowing there's no way I could've
    been so strong—so strong
        enough to carry a country

on my trapezius muscles,
    as if I were Sisyphus
        or Atlas, but really, more like

a real man, full-up on fire.

MODE FOR JACOB LAWRENCE'S "THE 1920'S...THE MIGRANTS ARRIVE AND CAST THEIR BALLOTS"

—"I never use the term 'protest' in connection with my paintings. They just deal with the social scene.... They're how I feel about things."—Jacob Lawrence

How I feel about things when I look at glowing brown faces of migrants who left the south to pull levers up north is how I feel about the propulsion of Black people born of blues and cutthroat salvation since realizing, "I am living for the next generation." How I feel about things is like I feel about being a cherry

blossom, extracting my scent and my plumes over everything for once because this spring is coming with a vengeance, and I am not the meek. I will not inherit this earth we love and hate on. Believe the words coming from this canvas. There will be no more keloid trees on brown backs, or the backs of brown

children. There are faces of promise on this canvas, canes for old legs, women with swollen pride and dead husbands, and new children who don't know no better because all they know is this breath— the one right now, where the honey is weak-thin, and the manna a smidge tougher than how they claim

it tastes in the old testament because nothing tastes the same when living in desperate time zones. The faces on this canvas look to pull levers like it will get them into the equality section of heaven. This canvas does not call it protest even when signing its John Hancock onto paper that will get it dead. It'll

run away, but it will run splat back into its own face. This here canvas ain't running. It's movement, and turning keloid backs into smooth brown skin. There is an incision in the souls on this canvas, and seeing it, sutures us new. Look at the faces. See the dark faces—the angel's loud-humming in Jacob's dreams.

MODE FOR FRIEND WHO USED TO BE A SKINHEAD & ASKED ME TO GO TO CHURCH W/ HIM

after taking my Introduction to Creative Writing class, and I thought about how
the air traveled around my ears like vespers from the mouths of the ash trees
and sycamores discussing the war on the emerald ash borer beetle, and how it

ate up family from the outside-in to the inside-out, as well as how far from Asia
and Eastern Russia they traveled to upset Indiana. In Indiana, in our Indiana, we
are like the splintered wood in the hollowed out trees, some tossed out bric-a-

brac of a moment where I see strange fruit hanging about the Hoosier diorama

and matrix of hate. But there we were, eyes break-dancing in the sunlight, giving
dap and fist bumps—brown and white skin honored to touch the other's, next to
smoking hut. How our grandfathers would see our solidifying functions as some

charlatan move in race relations. Is this far reaching or not reaching far enough,

in a state where Klan numbers rose to infinity? I see my voice lost like all the ash
trees. I see my voice lost in what the sycamore cares not to remember. In funnel,
my friend's voice got lost in soft echoes, where his mind misfired. I didn't attend

my friend's church. Not due to the who—the what he'd been. Our benevolence
took three steps forward and one step back—it rose above the backwash filling
our brains and made us climb to the top of real—the red-hot where blues festers.

MYTH (A TRUE STORY)

I was born from cold whispers of palsies &
plagues in graveyards, from cemeteries where
my life's chipped in carved names, a craft for
limestone, residents I never put my eyes on—
so old, I putty w/ their facts. Born w/out a head,
or feet, or hands—part something, part nothing.
I'm some kind of baby, some kind of religion.
Questions turn over like rust-color maple leaves,
become answers—become what's missing, the researched
something. *I am nobody; yet, everybody knows
my game.* I was born in an alley to an ally called

g h o s t—p o r t e n t. *What's new w/ dead?*

Dung eaters breathe under the icy wind circulating
& bending long lemon grass to the northeast,
their antennae tickling the torso, 6-feet under
an undercarriage, where dead things live. Undead
still, I articulate for skull & bone & the intangibles
I never put hands on. Still, I must release all their stuck moans.

WHEN YOUR MOTHER CORRECTS THE INDIANA POET LAUREATE you feel

like yelling, "No Miss Sofia!" as if you are Laurence Fishburne and she is Oprah Winfrey caught up in the past. Shame on your brown face like rouge. But a minute later, when he comes back to

her acknowledging she is correct, you realize she's always been correct, and although you never thought where you came from would matter much, a splash resides, and it all crests back to Lake Michigan washing up on your life, and how you would one day butterfly into a man with legs, ma-

triculate into another day to flap your wings. To never know you'd meet a man who would become

your bookmark. A man who would become your eye-loop. A man who would become another man in front of you—a voice you recognize in the wolf's howl. Some say you should have never been

here, but you have always leaned on stargazing and letting the moon burn its lips on yours. Somehow you saw the moment your mother would meet the Indiana Poet Laureate, and somehow you were al- ways here, and he would be all these men packaged like lunchmeat into some moment of time where

you have swallowed life like bites of tart green apple in the backyard of your suburban mess. The

yard, your mother built a garage on. The world's a small place full of eyeballs for huge moments. You wish more brain matter, but your head hits the mesosphere driving out of the county of lakes—

everything behind you is closer than it seems. You still go forward, into the darkness, where a white line pulls you back to where you'll start propulsion, again. Although the world is not a circle, it is an O-shaped mouth yawning in the hurt of morning sun on its walk of shame. Most times you end up

somewhere you have faded out, but begin where there's no footprints—torn edge of rotating beginnings.

BOXING ARETHAS
—thinking of the Queen of Soul

Sometimes the song brims too much power—
the voice dynamic, masterful like hieroglyphics

engraved in Giza pyramid. The timbre, reveling
like a son in his mother's smile, her sundress playing

street-games with the wind—the day's moon handling
her radiating skin. It's all too much, this rhythm

masking itself like the veil a nun inhabits, but is
more the skirt with the split up her leg that she wore

before believing there's a high life. To participate in
heaven and hell—yin and yang, the dualities we

must suffer. Like it all matters. The song, rotating
and turning on the record player, has too much power,

with its diamond needles and female grooves
of loves, of duties. Early Sunday afternoons are evil

when the song revolts, doesn't loom in luminance
like you like—doesn't give in to the tears that kamikaze

off your face, into the whiskey or wine—doesn't
glamorize the glitz and sexy of the morality of lunacy.

Here, there's a fist to the gut, the raw guttural quake
walking within you—a dark alley and one blinking light.

COMMUNION

We accepted psalms like kids accept bubblegum—

washed each other's feet, down below, in holy sanctuary, where God, in the dim
candle light, made me feel smaller than a granule. I wouldn't wash little sister's itty-
bitty pretty feet, but full up on the spirit, I washed off the bitterness of hammertoes,

gnarled pinky nails, the crusted corns of self-hate—soft like Magdalene's sighs, soft
like a summer's moon. In basement, males washed each other's feet. Females washed
each other's feet. "Saints" called *brother...sister,* "believers" that this world offers

an opulence to life: an indelible hour built on small seconds, rituals. No music—live
hummingbird voices praying real warm, engulfed in light. Always, it splashes back to

light in the darkness, in the midnight hour. Once a year, our hands created complete-
ness. *This* saved me, sanctified me through high school halls without impregnating
stupid girls, stupid and ripe like I was—a place I prayed and played a sad cornet for

God's choir. I wished an idyllic wish to *be* the path, to wash hard, ashy, feet, accept
my place as new spirit animal. Until sullied voices scarred ears; until I couldn't grasp
slippery soap in soapy water, replace ugly heart with cleanliness. Once, only a bare

smile. Once, a time so poor and free from made up.

SATURDAY MORNING'S STARFISH
AND COFFEE

—thinking on Prince

Once I saw a captured spider
dropped inside a toilet bowl.
When it hit that cool water—
a magical blossom of
little spiderlettes from inside
a mother's unseen sac.
How the "plop" sounded like
a Friday-night-gunshot.
How they scattered like Chi-town kids
do, when someone yells, "Gun!"
How they all twirled
like some circular cavalcade
around Esther Williams
in the film *Neptune's Daughter,*
until there was nothing
left after the funnelling hurricane
but whiteness and water,
and a voice that said "humh,"
like an off-stage Poseidon,
who never thought until
that moment, "What were
the children's chances
in their first minute to
this thing called life?"

THREE CHROMATICS
(SKINNY POEM TO FAT POEM)

i.

there is no more specific life
skin

god
purpose

beaten

skin
strange
bodies

own

skin
there is no more life specific

~~~
us apart from our bodies
action

house
gun

fear

action
skeletons
unspokens

bloodlines

action
our bodies apart from us

~~~
a pile of unspokens not reached
burnt

trees
crowing

racial

burnt
moths
flaring

melodies

burnt
piles of unspokens not reached

ii.

there is no more specific life
skin

sun-kissed by god
purposed

beaten like paste

skin
a strange want
bodies

to own

skin
there is no more life specific

~~~
us apart from our bodies
action

centuries in one house
gun

protect a fear

action
a pile of skeletons
unspokens

bloodlines

action
our bodies apart from us

~~~
a pile of unspokens not reached
burnt

hanging trees
crowing

racial

burnt
bodies of singed moths
flaring

melodies

burnt
piles of unspokens not reached

    iii.

there is no more specific life
as the skin we are in

melanin & sun-kissed by god
purposed like his christ-child

& beaten like paste into the earth

as the skin we are in
a strange mystery to want to tear
us apart from our bodies

the strange hands who want to own us

as the skin we are in
there is no more life specific

~~~
us apart from our bodies
an action from day one to next weekend

all these centuries in one house
now they only talk to us in gun

to protect a fear we never wore

an action from day one to next weekend
& there's a pile of skeletons
a pile of unspokens not reached

like a song planted in the bloodline

an action from day one to next weekend
our bodies apart from us

~~~
a pile of unspokens not reached
the momentum of voices burnt raw

the hanging trees
the jim crow bingo sheet

the post-racial fabrication

the momentum of voices burnt raw
our bodies singed moths
our minds flared mirages

our blood-stain melodies

the momentum of voices burnt raw
of unspokens a pile not reached

MAGIC TRICK (MAKING A SONG BRIDGE)

—for uncles & aunts

Babies feel rhythm's warmth
coming from within the cavity of
your mouth, when you beatbox

to get their bodies jumping,
while in your arms. They vigorously reach
inside, up to their elbow, wondering

how to capture the highs & lows.
It's like them Hungry Hungry Hippos
who want all them marbles. No,

it's like them frenetic crocodile-trainers
who embody *there's no life unless our hands
are tickling the tonsils of reptiles,*

or maybe it's the nephew's passion for that
last bite of sweet potato pie you pilfered & put
into your mouth—it's that the niece saw it,

& she wants it more—knowing booming
taste of pie crust, married to mama's 3-generations
of homemade filling, can get her slapped.

Nieces & nephews double-take, eyes jutting
at how you make music transparent from within
your talk-box. You feel their fingers

wiggle—reaching for trebles, all over
your taste buds, touching molars & tonsils &
the upper ridge of the soft palate, testing

your gag reflex for bass, until both of their
hands grab the top & bottom row of teeth, wanting
to stick their head within, like old lion tamers.

It's all in the eyes, when children look
back at you, baffled before smiling again, before
you bring hot beatbox back—laying down

how hip-hop births its on & on & on...

MEETING UP (COMING BACK FROM THE GREENER SIDE)

Things tangle in the stomach when the family meets.
This is the confessing, that old nigstalgia. Gray hairs

wave out of our aging naps, to the we we look back
to, the people we know we know. Sibling's voices,

laugh-crying crossways of me, discussing the orange
of Thursdays or that tincan taste of Mondays, and how

this act of confessing smacks. This could be the hurt
poem, but love singes so tough it suffocates like the 2nd

week in a nervous breakdown, and every crack on my
sibling's faces hurts me to look at. Still, I make it last.

We are so spread out—marbles watering out of bag.
Our voices scattered, old buck shots. Now, we sync up

to each other's ephemeral voice in our heads. Home,
our own dirty plot of land, where we're imploding about

Ma's homemade mac-n-cheese, odiferous memory of
trying to pick coconuts off her lemon cakes, or which

of her babies bent old truth on how her JFK 50¢ pieces
vacated. "Every piece of this place hurts me." *Leave her*

unspoken? You can't let time slosh around. It is all I
have to connect myself to my past. *You don't leave*

projects unless dead, or w/ scars—keloids of the brain.
In the backpack on my heart are the tinkles tingling me.

This confession is worn so tightly, I love the choking.
Misdirected by a new teat, we still taste the sweet of 1st.

On this side of fence, we live w/ how we cleared barb-
wire, but no escape. The poor we left, muscling us back.

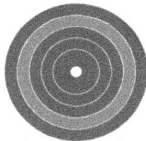

The Grey Singles

HEY MAN (A SHOUT OUT)

—for stuart scott (july 19, 1965-january 4, 2015)

it's been a minute since we held laughter down & tickled her anger,
since we hung our individuality on clotheslines for summer freshness,
since we helped failure up out of that impermeable gravel,
            since then, it's been a bit of this, that

it's been a minute since we picked up distraction on our last road trip,
since those tuesdays we tied up ad hominems at political campaigns,
since you showed me how to ride appendiceal cancer w/ a childhood saddle,
            since then, it's been a little this, a little that

i should've hit you up when you told me loneliness tried slipping you rohypnol,
since we hadn't eaten turkey burgers w/ sweet potato fries in a month of Sundays,
since the saturday we played touch-football on your manicured yard w/ those badass kids,
            since then, it's been a little bit of this, & a little bit of that

although it's been a minute since a *boo-yah*, i'm still a boo-yah baby,
since there's no *as cool as the other side of the pillow* falling like peaceful cinders
since there's no miracle of high-top fades anchoring on how grown folks play,
            since then...since then, there's been glitches...

for who will *check-ball* the establishment,
let the sharpness of street verbiage shower onto old school migraines
& flutter about in the madness like air particles on currents?

            i just needed to say *hey* back to the last message you left on this phone
            i just needed to say *hey* back to the last message, you...
            stu, i just needed to say *hey*

PDAS

This is a poem born in '91,
  from 1st Gulf War, where Fort Wayne
    Police Officer was jittery in airport terminal.
      Anticipation and family waited with him,

    for Buck Private on leave from search
  for Saddam. When young black soldier
held his brother in I-won't-let-go-embrace,

  I saw their arms
    full muscled—tension bands. War tick-tocked—
      a tiny man in my heart kicked me with steel-toed
    appreciation, sending bell to the top, ringing my
  throat with a dry thick burn churning gulp.

Tears did what they do. I wrote, *Would cop see*
  sibling in 6 months? Two black men uniformed
    for service, in context, in so perfect proportion
      one won't make it back to his distant childhood.

    So *leave* meant remembering and remembering
  has brought me back to when I stood up,

had infant poem down
  on paper. Spoke, "I know you don't know me
    but this is for you. It's a poem 'bout brothers.
      Take it, please." They took it, looked frozen
    like sane people do with crazy.

  I walked for exit, avoiding the Kodak flash,
but here I am, again, arms tight about it.

10 YEARS LATER...INTO *THAT* TUESDAY

(War Cry)

i.

Clean-shaven, a priest stands in green grass troubled about arch diocese:
    pedophilia, gay parishioners, and female clergy wannabes

A lady in tan Capri pants holds her daughter's hand so tightly light won't
    penetrate between them and no man will debauch the enforced bond

On Shyrock's Auditorium steps brown faces play drums,
    an antiquation of the Congo—new nostalgia of America

A news reporter from Channel 3 News has a mic shoved in her face
    her ululations feed-back anonymous fear

An Asian and blond in daisy dukes solicit female sex in a stream,
    we all want a fast love in brief blurs on hot roller blades

The drums are mad, belligerent, hacking out the mucous enflaming their throats

ii.

In heartland, family room for the south,
    townies aren't static they are activity,
    engaging; Dodge ramming, Ford tough, like a rock

iii

Here, each word is a life, a symbol in society
    and an unraveled paragraph trimmed out
    to look like a sentence—meager, means absence

iv.

Mama hands out stamps at post office—a woman handling my heart
    helps untaught kids in a library, hope—stuffed-shrimp swathe
    in Monterey Jack Cheese and Billy Wilder flicks cram my cranium

v.

Walking to my car, head stuffed w/ *ifs*, those babbling drums
    pulsate my brain (heel toe heel toe) and the screams
    are absent voices in bubbles, lifting, missing, listen...

WHEN PEOPLE LOSE EACH OTHER THEY TURN INTO BIRDS

—for Brettski

This is the drunk poem. A *Caw!Caw!Caw!* for an ingénue in a sundress chunk of s k y . She's a Cali girl, a ghetto bird dispersed, fumbling within the cross-

winds of suffocation —from L o n g B e a c h to Carbondale—her last flight to e a s t e r n lights. N o w , a Michigan babe dressed in funeral g a r b hugs

an Indiana dude dressed in f u n e r a l garb. Their arms adapt into w i n g s— no matter. They w i n g around each other's b o d y , a s t r a n g e c oo for

theC a l i girl born with S p a n g l i s h lungs.This is an a n e c d o t e poem, crash landing, trans f e r r i n g ghetto birds into humans who love humans—

no m a t t e r . Now, the babe & dude are ghetto birds. Ghetto birds l o v e ghetto birds, no matter. When ghetto birds cry, it s o u n d s like a train's

wheels s t e e l - b r a k i n g . This poem b r e a k s into a confetti-parade o f f e a t h e r s . So many feathers, they rumble in the sky's t h r o a t—   h e l i copter

down like live blades . So many feathers, ghetto b i r d s f e e l p a l t r y , but don't stride like c h i c k e n s—ghetto bird's are nasty-smooth, familiar

like r u m . E v e n if quietquills aresilent whentheyland,   the babe & dude listen. So   many s i l e n c e s ride on   this rain. This is w h y g h e t t o

b i r d s warble S e p t e m b e r . This is why California is their v e r b —no m a t t e r .

NIKO (NEE-KOH)

—thinking on Nick Meneakis

I recall your head on the chalkboard,
mouth giving us a sermon on how not

to leave our responsibility in the hands of
our loco sidekick, tragedy. Your hair fell

across your forehead like a willow tree
giving psalms. How jazzy those days,

where light shown on us through huge high
school windows. How calm your anger.

The son you lost. We were bad reps for
what children do to make parents cry for joy.

This music, chronic, and classic, building
and building as you made dots by hitting

the chalkboard with the chalk, keeping the beat,
while the dust fell about like snowflakes.

The hope, your sighs saturate into our craniums.
You pray for dumb luck, that anything can

saturate into the thickness of impenetrable
skulls. You took it until you couldn't take it.

Now, you are stuck in a plastic groove, in
the classroom in my cranium, where shit-

heads and dumbasses reside along with
the triggering smell of grandma's lattice

apple pies. You are mugging at my Nana,
whose silver hair is cleanly wrapped in

a bun. Your son is eating a slice of pie,
waving at me to come, to join the rhythmic

tableau of actors in musical for the dead.

IN DETROIT, DEAD MUSICIANS STILL KILL FOR A SET

~~~

The music penetrated the paintingsonthe   w a l l s
and the m a g i c voicesfromthe paintings blend
with the   v o i c e s at the o p e n - m i c j a m
s e s s i o n, and we a l l sweated,   smoldering
in the steam of hot cat fish, collards, and   baked
mac & cheese, adding   more fingerprints to
the stained menus. Wanting what other   patrons
at other tables smack on. E n t e r s a   dancing-
man leaning on metal cane.   He can't stop what
the d r u m m e r is aching at, what the b a s s
player's doing live and has bleeding fingers for,
what t h e Marvin Gaye cover guy is p u t t i n g
on us like a welt. It's D-town's r e constructi o n , and
the paintings on the walls , rum and coke   happy,
harmonizing until they s w e a t out *oh yeahs,*
hallelujahs,   and   *gawd   damns,* as
s t a c y adams, high   heels, and even the   broke
h a n d - m e - d o w n s s m a c k hard on the
b l a c k   and w h i t e tile like it's a   s w e a t y
woman's f i r m ass. "Oh   y e a h! It is!"

~~~

GHOST WALKER

—thinking on Steve Hollander

On Thursday, a man glided down the hall
of the Liberal Arts building, phosphorescent
in ectoplasm, but corporeal like you in
every bit of how you lilt. But it wasn't you.
You can't look like *you* when this is not the
old Classroom Medical building *you* troubled.
When *you* were here, living in *your*
thin frame, office full of books and papers
splattered all around like a condemned
library, *you* had to move through the halls
to get to something chocolate. The big Hershey
bar, bigger than your head, the best deal
to deal with in-the-ways: students, faculty,
administration. Every day there's a bomb
ready to explode. Every bite your teeth
sunk into sweet oblivion. I think you, when
I see huge candy bars calling me in Walgreens.
But today, I hadn't thought you, until
the man in his thin frame, with haggard
beard, walked in the-language-of-hummingbird
towards me. I saw a flicker—threw a smile,
threw a fervent hello. He was gruff-gruff,
and didn't return any change. I go into my
office using sighs. You would never pass
me wearing gruff. You would sit in my office,
complain about how my organization's odd.
How there are not enough stacks of student
papers: "things to be done this week,"
"things to be done next week," and "things
for later." But you wouldn't live long in
that brawling. You would grub down
the Swiss bar in eye shot, and laugh
at my transparency halting your howling
at education making your bones clack
with your mouth full of rich creamy globs—
the swallowed mmms; the raw moans.

RICHARD PRYOR AND ME

It's a feeling of holiday inside,
'cause every time I'm with you
you aren't funny, have less pressure
to be that rocket on stage, breaking us
into two with those cut-'em-up skills
God signed you on for. When we're
rappin' I only hear your hurt shatter
like Bird sellin' another sax for smack,
knowin' he gon' be back to get his
love-baby mellow soother—knowin'
he got bills, and women, and music
to support and spoon. When it's us,
Rich, rappin' and talkin' 'bout how Bad
got us in trouble growin' up—we'll both
tell each other we didn't have to follow
Bad but he had a way of gettin' into us
gut. He'd puff his cheeks on harmonica,
get dizzy with his looseness for trouble,
and we'd come runnin'—he didn't have
one smooth Coltrane note in him. Nawh,
he'd play a cutthroat-crossroad-sweetness
and we loved to chat and shoot our wads
with that fallin' angel, 'cause we knew
how if he had bones they'd rattle like ours
and he'd love the pain he'd feel for being
human, unlike us—scared to love big,
to follow our insanities. We try to hide
in our botched prayers, want only good
things, things appealing to the eyes
of others, stuff we hope to handle
on the run, and things big, red,
popped bright in glare.

HYPOCRITICS

It's much harder to pick out the vegetarian zombies,
    laboring across the screen   like the liver eaters. Still,

I take on the gig. I do it just to see agony ride their
    faces with irony. One points   her raggedy finger towards

the moving meat. In close frame, I see all of her deteriorations
    as she screeches about midnight.   *How can you yell without*

a voice box? But she does. *Such is zombie life, I guess.*
    Another's good at grabbing   ankles, feet. He bites a bit,

but spits back out the vibrating flesh because even in this
    state he feels like a hypocrite.   Another gets caught

because it's all too much, this dying and reawakening
    and hunger for each morsel   you never even wanted.

THE NEED FOR BOTTLED WATER

—*International nuclear regulators warned Tuesday that growing amounts of radioactive water in and around Japan's tsunami-stricken Fukushima Daichi nuclear power plant remained a threat and said it must be disposed of responsibly. (NBCnews.com)*

our water you can't even boil,
    mixed with radiation and the suffering

brain-patterned marks of hiroshima.
    we can't give our children those memories

tied to a new madness. in japan,
    fathers only want to *quench our child's*

thick thirst. in japan, a mother wants to
    do what mothers have done since mothers

have been mothers—*give alms, souls to this*
    earth, but japan has split up its own body,

has become a newsworthy magic trick, which
    leaves backwash of haiti of sichaun of katrina

in each blessed slurp and gulp from plastic bottles
    handled by red-cross and other relief-funded

violin players. *nothing's the best way.* so tap-
    water carries with it jinx-guilt, or something

that stains raw like a rorschach splotch
    in our brain. as *our terra turns itself inside*

out, simultaneously the unrighteous
    and righteous work to relieve, but look

how compassion rides on guise in the dead
    eyes of correspondent focusing on sore ruin

under her feet, searching our capacity for hate, but
    we meld, move back to our *sweet ebb to flow.*

LICKING THE SALT IN OCEAN AIR MODE

—for Mellie Mel and Roxy

(1) *There are women born California who dream*
they will own oceans for life. They discover *this* from
French kisses—scratches on a bad boy's back. Dreams.

It's through dreams and the momentum of why dreams
slam into their brains—conducting waves to walk into

a reality, a purpose—the hand touching underneath
black lace bra, not squeezing the breast but caressing

the beat, searching life's bulges, praying for wisdom
that arcs above the head. When the woman *here* designs

like woman sifting grain on archipelago, in adobe
kitchen, the "Me! Me! Me!" is a hand reaching for all.

(2) *Sometimes it's a splayed hand spreading over her*
heart until she can feel dim throb of his heartbeat
pulsing with hers, saying, "I only want tomorrows."

But for those who've never licked the salt in ocean
air, it is a smoke-and-mirror pony-trick. No one

can manhandle constellations. We all have been
burned to a recognition that our scars are smoldering

palisades only reachable by dark seagulls. When
the rain plat plat plats, concrete timbre moans,

sounds out birth noun, Pasadena. In Southern Cali
these women allege loyalty to this dream, pulsating—

but we all lie for a reality, each second, this must.

COMMISSIONED

"You look as good as the artwork,"
her breath hits him, raising the eyebrows

of two friends flanking her. Tipsy is
what she is. A hook-up. And he sees her

clothes on his floor in that part of mind
we are not to speak out loud about.

His girlfriend will rage-wild if he sexes
up some situation looking to have something

up in her from his dark mass. *She's trolling.*
So he just smiles, adjusts himself,

his demeanor on how *upper class chicks think*
they can have anyone and anything by

showing they aren't wearing any panties.
He has been there, done them, and is

more worried about how his words will
harmonize with the glasswork of William

Morris. Will words glisten with the glass's
shine of black crow beaks and canopic jars?

Or will it all go to shit—the tweets
will be of a dark poet who is out of his

assigned box, trying for tier-one rankings of
those nibbling Brie, drinking Chardonnay,

inside atrium of the Fort Wayne Museum?
The wine-drunk with flirt on her breath

says nasty things with her smile, pushing
grunts in air. In a crowd, he loses her, moves

to outskirts, to rush to the rustling rustlers,
to think on Hurston, Toomer, Van Der Zee—

hear the ancestors boycott about in his head.
My mother. My sister. My woman.

A sweet and painful smile manipulates his face.
He feels old hands on his soul, knows those

who walked dirt roads also paves him.

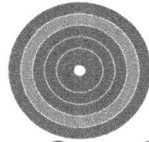

Living in the Grey Matter Cento

LIVING IN THE GREY MATTER CENTO

before us, bodies giving up their last holy word.
i once sat in the same moment too—

there is an incision in the souls on this canvas,
    and i'm begging god for another two minutes.

we all have been burned to a recognition
that our scars are smoldering palisades—

eyes break-dancing in the sunlight,
    ongoing into an aria, spent in the ether

of alphabetic limbo—an o-shaped mouth
yawns in the hurt of morning sun, and

    in the smallness, we get to know now.
        ###

so many silences ride on this rain—
saturate into the thickness of impenetrable skulls.

the music penetrated, blooming out of his afro.
every day there's a bomb ready to explode—

circular watermarks from neglected drinks. *listen...*
we try to hide in our botched prayers,

hungry for each morsel. two bodies swim
within orgasm. the trees have cried

their leaves to the ground
and made us all fly.
        ###

the lime stench of the city—
    the streets strayless, glistening with

the glass's shine of black crow beaks—
    rankling moans of ghosts lie faint in the distant,

searching night for another new god—
    jumping crystals before halogen car lamps.

hot-pins prickle skin—handled by red-
    cross and other relief-funded violin players.

our voices scattered, old buck shots—
    burdened and marred w/ fragments—

throat surrounded in wool.
    inside, the aging us,

smaller than a granule, this
    life in the next quadrant of existence.

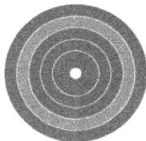

Top 10 Greyz

FOR YOU (MR. NELSON)

The day before Minnesota found you splayed out,
like some master's painting under another

  painting we knew nothing about
    until museum authorities investigate,

you made grand plans for elsewhere-
&-other-things. Death hit you w/

  a ninja's punch—left you, evaporating like smoke
    & doubt. & you probably took a few more steps

in your million-dollar high-heels, coordinating
w/ your badass couture—wrapped around your little

  body, before wondering about losing balance—
    that balance you always wear—a sure-foot

like JB gliding in his black ankle-boots &
pencil-legged slacks—sliding into nevuh-evuh.

  & on the floor inside your paisley elevator,
    in your palatial color of royalness, there's one

thought, "Damn, I'm not gone make it to the next-
thing-&-that." So when we heard about you,

  displayed like a swanky Picasso, we thought it
    one of those internet-mismanaged-hoaxes,

or a new Prince-game you'd play to capture
our united focus. & only if it were.

I'M SINGING THIS POEM FOR YOU (DRAFT #33)

—for the Hathaway daughters

I dream up some sweet days even ya'll didn't
own, a number on Santa's list. Your dad warms
us at Christmas, cools us of summer's mean—
his lyrics christening in us a crystalline therapy.
You held him in the everyday, throughout year—
even when he was dematerializing (he played
notes, snuggled): leaving hung shirt, a toy, kiss
he called brown sugar spread on your face like
some viral love, but then he evaporated, leaving
the boy of him clacking in your head like bell
from corner church bell-tower, lone metronome;
he cried melody on your pillow, by hungry ears—
an unlikely likeness—an only dream you can
only share on the Sabbath, on knees to Yahweh.
And still there's no able phrase to pray from
the mad to the sweet. He owned his angels, his
demons, all spinning ghetto merry-go-rounds—
in center of centripetal force his undizzy voice—
the *real deal*, how angels chanted matins God
commanded, but those demons were nasty crab-
grass in his beautiful garden under large apple
cap; you three, sweet lotuses blooming out of
his afro—streaming in a sweat, releasing toxic
demonic runoff—so his lotuses could breath—
so his lotuses could glow, become new jujubes.

HOMAGE TO THE GOOD FOOT

—for the Godfather of soul

The first time I saw your skinny legs
in those slim lined tapered black slacks,
you were shaking like mixing prongs in
Mama's cake batter. You were kicking it
with Frankie Avalon and his beach buddies
on a movie set where skiing and snow are
like an Elysian Fields for the lighter brother.
My home was a project townhouse in Gary,
and my sister and I laughed at how many

ants must be biting on your black ashy legs,
in them tight pants. You shut us up, glided on
one foot to the left for about two days, and
then to the right to finish out southern equator.
And hacky horns split atoms like pecans
or peanut shells, clacking between two forces
pushed against each other—bodies blown to

pop. That's "The One," where band grabs
the mane of a blaring black stallion and rides
out its melody—and the hooves are piss hot,
and the white kids jerk like they'll break their
necks on the one and three. You owned me.
I jumped off Mama's bed, and my little sister
jumped to floor too, and in our dingy socks
we slid on our bare floor, and stepped on ants
to discover which of our feet had you down.

SATURDAY NIGHT HYPNOCRITE

—after Michael F. Patterson

he walk around all jazz, when he really a trouble man screaming like he a detroit-sweet afro, sliding out between his band-mates for his solos. but he born of mill-steel, hoosier, a cardinal shaking its red tail-

feather, a concrete-street-geek. his pavement, street shoes in motion. songs lodged in esophagus. big mama thornton riding his gut. how he got it, he stole it like a stick-up-kid of blues, car- jacking the foot-

steps of life. he walk around all jazz, when he really funk-defied, the sun his mama put in the sky to light up his mind. he is the blue light, the red light, the daylight of lost souls. he is that base- ment smell in all

after parties, that double-check of underarms. he is the piss and moan of snake eyes and running bostons the nights before the fight for the morning, before the fight of putting on his sunday's best to listen

to the signifying preacher and the city's best choir, many who lost their bank to him. he walk around, all jazz, but gravel rattles in his kicks, rattles like the loose change in pockets that he pilfers from collection.

WHERE I'M AT

Where was I when Louis and Duke
were skating the town on blue note
vibrations? Why couldn't I brush up
against all the music happening at
The Savoy or The Audubon—bump
into Dutch Schultz at the Cotton Club
or Bumpy chatting with the Nicholas
Brothers, where music lived? Death,
no music. Why was I born so late in
this existence where the music pops
in and pops out? I have too many
questions about atmosphere and where
I am supposed to land. What's great is
my depression and longing for *my* place
in the history of a scat-man-scatting.
There are too many notes from those
roaring twenties and Harlem jam
sessions—living-rooms where Bix
and Louis could play outside of racism.
It was the music transforming dreams.
My dreams laze in blues, jass, swing
notes that bring me home, a dog with
intrinsic pattern of pictures in brain:
flash cards. I know hurt in Armstrong's
smile, it ain't blue, it's ongoing into
an aria of light. The sweaty women—
the women waving and shaking their
shimmies to genius of how blackness
upsurges coal white spirit: a Basin Street
bruise, a West End bruise—happiness
caught in down, sweet need to get back
up. The air so thick with sixteenths,
a hot music handling suckers for babes.

IMOJEAN GABLE'S street ballerina, unveiling the thorns and thatches of real-ALITY

Dancing in a circle/ motions of lifemaking/ slight maneuvers
pausing in space

Replica of Salome, dancing in silence

Abandoned w/ ostracized notes/ alone/ around life

Everyday People move to evade her wretched raggedness

Wrinkled/ cracked/ head covered by a blue bandana, she shows
the Everyday People her naked, half-eclipsed smile

Dancing, humming, and darting furiously to piercing trumpet/
dunt DUN-nunt dunt DUN-nunt dunt DUN-nunt

They look through her seeing each other

Hearing childlike chuckles

A crowd of HE SAYS SHE SAYS

Dizzy's jive splits an atom

Be'boppin' w/ Birdland harmonies/ dunt DUN-nunt dunt DUN-
nunt dunt DUN-nunt be-Sha bop whopp be-Dow

Jean's lips form a circle

17 again, old lady dancing around her buggy, 17th and
Broadway

Dancing in a circle

Taking time to traffic/ jam

BOOMBOX HEAD

—for Hoodnick

You the mix-tape soundtrack singin your unspoken—
    the playback sloshin home to our city on the grind. It grinds on

us that "you don't leave Gary w/out keloids, prayers put up, or death."

What tinkles trickles back to a stale mechanical drawin classroom,
    where Mr. Olson's monotone bounced off our noncommittal

ears, where we jones'd 'bout life in the next quadrant of existence,

bankin on some grace after teenager. Old days sketch you the simile,
    like rooted tributary—light-skinned & testosterone-pampered in

perspiration, kickin Hendrix & Rotten in that heavy R&B zone, needin

a bed to rest your raw worries. Words could do you no harm. Binary
    colors of permanence never fit correctly. You spittin alternative

before it crashed couture—acceptin the screech from cats caught tails.

We were deaf mostly, slapped by history's backhand, stuck searchin for
    our parent's costumes to fit us. We traipsed not to be cardboard

replicas. "Not 'til we can accept how we must grow into the-our-selves-

we-never-see does the ON-switch click." You left Hoosier w/ your fro &
    toothy grin, hit Cali to never be the one of us missin the rapture—

fond of a chick named Blondie, a babe w/ black heart, tattooed Joan.

DIVAISM (DREAMING GRACE JONES)

Inside her fussing he stood up,
    with Cortés, looking for more

a greedy conquistador captain
    recognition that he had the cojones

to take from the unsuspecting,
    to control things over-the-top, but

more recognition he owned how
    his insides loosed like half-n-half

into black coffee, a soaking slush of
    mouth like Diego Rivera connecting

white gold. He lost his name in her
    more to Frida between thighs of her

sister. They shook, tongued, stroked
    moonlights, really only dreamable

eyes through an infantry of twenty
    minutes, playing with how darkened

body parts react to centripetal motion.
    stinging, soothing, then balming with

They washed each other of exchanges:
    lotion. Each other's private shavings

shining so fine black hair tricked them
    there, clambering down to slumber.

it could be light. He made mistake
    Her angry buttocks up—she, tight-

lipped at door—kissed him—talked on
    he'd been butted by. Glistening,

her cell—the best multitasking
    naked, she grabbed his movement,

readjusted how to make him big and small
    left him in her scent,

before her deep Good night Dad-dy shut door,
    aromatic grass on his top lip.

FENDER STRATOCASTER'S CONFESSION ON THE BLUES MAN

it was the raspy voice of hollow leg earl's lust that brought me to my last ecstasy with tolerance, & to question god. i was a neophyte, close to acoustic, but more in tone & timbre.

presence? i had no in-the-moment. hollow built me up w/ scales & stretches & scratches from handmade metal picks raising barfly's dead dreams. the cruelest work i got came from

dime-bags of back breaking unforgiveness, the hand-me-down in wrong, the spoon-fed po' from broken string to strum-&-twang in don't-want-to-even-sit-in-here establishments:

from abilene to mississippi, from 'bama to chi-town. for meals i got balm. still, grumpy hollow leg plucked me w/ calloused fingers of want. & i wanted to want. hollow pimped me out to

please. & i pleased the raspy cancerous voice of hollow leg. our call & response in a house full w/ drunks got standing-o's. but like tina w/in ike's menagerie, tears have stained my body

like circular watermarks from neglected drinks. listen, it's not all on hollow. my octaves did veer west. but ya'll say music killed him. & ya'll never see the grooves he left under my buffing.

SONG OF THAT DAMN OLD HOUSE (A GHAZAL)

I got caught, snagged on yesterday's jagged bones.
Your supernova explodes in my mind, shatters bones.

You rub your eyes, loosen filament—a matrimony replacing
our song on IPod with the blues: "Thrummin' Bones."

I'm sand-sad, magma rock—trinkets stuck in Mother's earth.
The archaeologist of love lost the path to our bones.

My mother placed prayers on her bedroom shelf, in God's reach.
God balms Mama's regret with blaze for family's bones.

It's the season to plant bulbs—pull up tap roots—spray bugs.
Bug larvae full of pus organs—all white—no bones.

Your letters were the last time I thought in chrysanthemum.
Then, love was our home. My fingertips trace a phantom's bones.

FANATICS FOR GENIUS

They all walked in the smoke, ethereal
and visceral, arms length away. They have
carried us on high notes, under low ceilings,
when comatosed. The prophets, the Satchmos,

the Helen Kellers, and the Einsteins. It's all
moon glow, chrysanthemums, jumpy pomposity
of Dionysus—inconspicuous as dawn, a light
panther's stalking. We doubt what we doubt—

ourselves in neon light of the milieu. In breaker-
box, light comes alive, fused by genius inklings
and complex tumblers of inventors who patent
the neo, the post-, a nouveau. They get us through

moments we remember we never would profess.
A note is more than a note, more than a splotch
on a scale. The gold in genius is that goal

stretching to genius. "I'd do wrong for you,
baby." A body sacrifices itself, Mama's morals,
to play naked in nightclubs of loud drinkers,
smokers, and men and women begging each

other—dancing background of harmonies.
Why do the rankling moans of ghosts lie faint
in the distant as any sure refuge? We grab less,
crave unattainable, but hold what's unmeasurable.

When doors close, voices fade into cracks—
the architect's handcrafted molding. We hear
what we hear, what we always have with us,
the insalubrious rattle bucking our bones.

SUMMER TUESDAY

The rain slaps the roof, the windows, and the concrete. This music...this music, given to us like a glass of water, as we thirst like summer's flowers begging for psalms. I am lost

and found all at once. I am in a Burt Bacharach song. I am in a Temptation song. I have become a song. I am hitting the roof, the window, and the concrete, and something in me

splats but does not break. I have become water, fully. The rain and I are one now. We sit down on shingles and talk, slide down gutters, slide into the dirt with grubs and snails. Slide

into the street so car tires spin us into more puddles. What is this? I do not ask, I move. I move because there are no rules to being slippery. I move because there is no way to

escape this moment that flushes its clarity onto my face like a refreshing blast of want. The rain slaps the roof, the windows, my face. Such music, this. Such music...such music.

MILLENNIAL'S REQUIEM

Boomerangers not talking up
American dreaming. Not breathing

out the vowels their parents laid
like Easter eggs, into their ears,

in the canals to their minds. They are
owed things: college, security, a magical

wealth. They're born with DNA of

attrition. They're born with T-ball,
parental missteps, a fist called fairness.

The cantos of their life germinate
into a tangible dripping faucet,

crimson droplets. & since red don't
flow from their young veins,
                    the
                        youth
                            just
                                chilling
                            until
                        their
                parents
        take
            to
                the
                    grave.

The Grey 12-inches

@---

"How his mommy passed away, but these lines she used to say
  And at that time he couldn't understand

  And mama used to say..."

...you won't understand what i'm telling you now, but one day you will "move mountains. stomp mole hills. righteous glory born to. you from stellar backs. steel workers, postal workers, and soldiers garnered you titles in this. united states of e pluribus unum." booker t. and dubois ain't helping with these bills, and you eat a hell of a lot. listen now and hear me then. you need to learn to motivate. push the pulse, inspire. either matriculate or get job. but be more than one buck.

...one day i will release. let hand go. let you roam your own mind. "let hand go?" let me roam in my own bewitchment. i never learn release. keep hold of all. magnets. pics. refrigerated. freezing business. embracement. crash landing. splat on. face. sliding. frowns.

... "gotta find me an angel" with aretha, but really quilted in a ziggy patois with her mama, marie. laid to best. torqued to heartbreak. as aretha burns with her sister, carolyn. mama burns from the cortex of a nucleus. a light. lissom heaven. sound waves to ears. the burrowing down to gutbucket. ruddy.

... "if you want a do-right-all-day-woman, you gotta be a do-right-all-night-man" with aretha. again. vacuuming. again. dusty dustmites out darkened darkness. oblivion. that moment inside crevice. of her absolution. against blue collar husbands painting old school. convo. vaporizing off her clothes. men's red public eyes. search for new worth. a new position. passion. lurking for lust. here she gave me a solid moan. how not to sag manhood.

...you must open the door to enter yourself. i waited 20 years. in the basement of. my want for need. her hair tight on her. head. her skull illuminating parcels of grenadine. her mouth wrapped around glow vowels. god. i saw god. for one institution falls. for one institution stands. windows. doors. all to house. the empty. filled.

...most people are decent. with all the evil in world...never retracting. just dangling, on hang.

"A small boy once asked, When will I grow up
  When will I see what grownups do see..."

i am holding out. to hold on. my mother's dream. my mother's pride. a city's son. the bow. the arrow. some kemet god. engaged. odd. cocky. tight. locked.

now mama's words ricochet/boomerang my skull. my bones. fatherhood. i've stepped into some soupy resistance. mama's words are all on the soul of my blues. blue muddiness. i can't define.

i am nat love on a barren ranch of my forefathers. in my mind. learning…i am mishkinakwa looking at the clouds of my ancestors wave back to the migrating buffalo. searching…for i am. i am apple. moved from the original garden to uprooted earth. everyone takes. the bite.

when young, mama loco moto. at me. all in my grill bout. future. bout past. now future is a shirt. a yesterday. a today. i am all in me. to find i am her. defacto. whispers warm. the strange channels a voice carries on. the god in my head. jasmine. bulging nostrils. i came out a god. screaming psalms. no father.

she'd have rain whisked inside. head. saturdays. sloshing. always saturdays. sloshing. beloved because she breathes. the mist coming through window. the cooling language. from the voice. radio phonic pump of juicy. pulp. pulsing. pulsing. pop. rainfist. hitting concrete. hitting hurt where hurt could. not ride. summer rain flowers. cools sweat. our unconditioned lives. how we wait. for rain. blows.

i do not slide backwards. move. fall. forward down scraps the mind. behind me so much of what's behind me. i do not spiral. like spigot time in my radius. so close to the edge of grass. i am about. to the dream. spot. spitting. distance. come here. god's voice. shines.

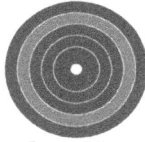

Living in the Greyz (Redux)

LIVING IN THE GREYZ REDUX

flutters like air particles on currents of new sound-
tracks busting beats

i retraced the steps
of your voice—

i am breathing in the day's anaphoras about unarmed boys
called vultures with busted wings.

a strange coo for
the cali girl born with spanglish lungs

i retraced the steps
of your voice—

into your diva self, give us a taste—
broken words scattering on lined expectations

with that fallin' angel, 'cause we knew
how if he had bones they'd rattle like ours

i retraced the steps
of your voice—

into its vortex, up to spaceship of love,
a wet promising in parking lot,

you crossed ocean with family, sat in the hot
seats of travel, give alms, souls to this

earth—those lips are worth all

i retraced the steps
    of your voice—

how can you yell without
    a voice box?—from the bottom

and top of the throat, full of cicadas
    and crickets enacting the day's concert—

life boomerangs back the manure needed for planting
    lullabies growing into tomorrow-things

i retraced the steps
    of your voice—

real motion gaining forward
    balance with each wobbly step—

stacy adams, high heels, and even the broke
    hand-me-downs smack hard on the

black and white tile
    online, when looking for new shoes

i retraced the steps
    of your voice—

legs are like pistons—how arms help momentum
    and the breath ghosting away rises into the night,

like train smoke—
    hydraulics and switches, a bumping system

how you would one day butterfly into a man
    with legs, matriculate into another day

to flap your wings

    i retraced the steps
of your voice—

    recall your head on the chalkboard,
mouth giving us a sermon

    i retraced the steps
of your voice—

    this music, chronic, and classic,
building and building

    i retraced the steps
of your voice—

    the orange of thursdays
or that tincan taste of mondays

    i retraced the steps
of your voice—

and the bitchy ache of day

i retraced the steps
    of your voice—

i retraced the steps
    of your voice—

i retraced the steps
    of your voice—

undead,
    still free to articulate all the old stuck moans

i retraced the steps
    of your voice—

the fallin out of the sky on my head
    into the matriarchal sundress of

rhythm that beats underneath your eyes

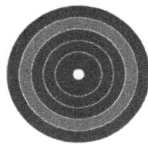

NOTES

(page 15) "The Burning Dance Lesson" is for "Tata," a.k.a. Nelson Rolihlahla Mandela. He went to jail for 27 years to help abolish apartheid as an activist. He later became the first president of South Africa, and won major awards like the Nobel Peace Prize and the Presidential Medal of Freedom. R.I.P. (July 18, 1918-December 5, 2013).

(page 23) "three chromatics (skinny poem to fat poem)" was inspired by the Skinny Poem. "The Skinny is a short poem form, created by Truth Thomas, that consists of eleven lines. The first and eleventh lines can be any length (although shorter lines are favored). The eleventh and last line must be repeated using the same words from the first and opening line (however, those words can be rearranged). The second, sixth, and tenth lines must be identical." The first segment of "three chromatics (skinny poem to fat poem)" takes on this formatting. More can be found at https://theskinnypoetryjournal.wordpress.com/2016/11/13/chromatics-by-curtis-l-crisler/.

(page 42) "the need for bottled water" addresses the threat of radioactivity still within Fukushima's water: http://www. nbcnews.com/news/world/fukushima-fallout-radioactive-water-remains-threat-iaea-says-n307361.

(page 55) "For You (Mr. Nelson)" plays off of Prince Rogers Nelson's first album, *For You*. R.I.P. June 07, 1958-April 21, 2016.

(page 59) In "Where I'm At" the reference to "Bix" refers to the jazz cornetist and pianist Leon Bismark "Bix" Beiderbecke, and who went by Bix Beiderbecke.

(pages 70 & 77) @ includes excerpts from the song "Mama Used To Say," by the singer-songwriter Junior. He was born Norman Washington Giscombe on June 6, 1957. "Mama Used to Say" was recorded in 1981 and released as a single in the UK in 1982 from his album *Ji*. Junior Giscombe and Bob Carter wrote the song.

(page 73) The poem, "gotta find me an angel," was inspired by aretha franklin's song "angel," which was originally released on June 2, 1973, by Atlantic, and written by Carolyn Franklin and Sonny Saunders.

(page 74) The poem, "if you want a do-right-all-day-woman, you gotta be a do-right-all-night-man" was inspired by Aretha Franklin's song "do right woman, do right man" (written by Chips Moman and Dan Penn), and originally released on February 10, 1967 as the b-side to "I Never Loved a Man (The Way I Love You) written by Ronnie Shannon.

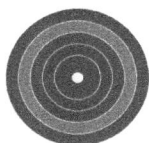

ACKNOWLEDGEMENTS

This manuscript could not have come to fruition without the fellowship from the Virginia Center for the Creative Arts (VCCA), the Individual Artist Program (IAP) grant from the Indiana Arts Commission (IAC), and my summer residency at the City of Asylum/Pittsburgh (COA/P) for their finances and space to help develop the book that my manuscript has become. All were instrumental in supporting my research and vision with this creative endeavor. Also, I would like to thank the artists at VCCA, who were there during my residency, and who gave me gracious feedback and insight on the manuscript (you are more than you know), and also the affiliation Cave Canem has with COA/P (thx CC for this).

I extend special gratitude to Finishing Line Press for publishing the chapbook *Soundtrack to Latchkey Boy,* and where part of *Soundtrack to Latchkey Boy* appears (section "The Grey Album 12-inches"). Also, I extend special gratitude to the following entities where my poems first appeared in some form: *Artisan* for "Imojean Gable's." *Atticus Review* for featuring me and my work: "mOde for friend who used to be a skinhead & asked me to go to church w/ him," "In Detroit, Dead Musicians Still Kill for a Set," "Licking the Salt in Ocean Air mOde," "Richard Pryor and me," and "Marrow." BAQ (Black Arts Quarterly) for "Where I'm At." *Bop, Strut, and Dance: A Post Blues Form for New Generations* (forthcoming) for "McLaren Rocks his Dome." Chris Rice Cooper's Blogspot where the essay "Formulating resis-stance" showcases "PDAs" and "10 Years Later... into *that* Tuesday." "10 Years Later...into *that* Tuesday" a.k.a. "that tuesday (war cry)" was first published in a community anthology in Carbondale, IL called *Voices for Peace.* *Copper Nickel: A Journal of Art and Literature* for "I'm singing this poem for you (draft #33)." *Delaware Poetry Review* (forthcoming) for "For You (Mr. Nelson)." *IndianaHumanites.Org/Think-Read-Talk* for "Singing her Augusta Savage mOde," a.k.a. "Singing Her Augusta Savage." *Map Points* for "Divaism." *Not Like the Rest of Us: An Anthology of Contemporary Indiana Writers* for "When your mother corrects the Indiana Poet Laureate you feel like yelling." *PLUCK* for "Meeting up (coming back from the greener side)" and "saturday night hypnocrite." *Re)verb* for "Fanatics for Genius." *Say it Loud: Poems about James Brown* for "Homage to the good foot." *Songs for a Passbook Torch* (anthology) forthcoming for "The Burning Dance Lesson." *The Indianapolis Review* (forthcoming) for "Boombox Head." *"The Skinny" Poetry Journal* for "chromatics," the first segment in the poem "three chromatics (skinny poem to fat poem)." *Undead: A Poetry Anthology of Ghouls, Ghosts, and More!* (forthcoming) for "Niko (Nee-koh)." *Valley Voices: A Literary Review* for "mOde for Jacob Lawrence's "The 1920's...The Migrants Arrive and Cast Their Ballots" a.k.a. "mOde for looking at the faces in 'The 1920's...The Migrants Arrive and Cast Their Ballots.'"

Tom C. Hunley, Steel Toe Books, and Western Kentucky University, there are no words. Thanks to George Kalamaras, Ross Gay, Mitchell L. H. Douglas, Christine Kincaid, Leah Maines, and Timeca Seretti for their immeasurable feedback, assistance, and encouragement. Love and honor to my family, friends, activists, publishers, IPFW English & Linguistics Department, IPFW faculty and students, the Indiana Chitlin Circuit, the Fort Wayne community and northeast Indiana, and the future movers and shakers I've worked with while developing this manuscript. U aLL R DiaMoNDS & PeaRLS.

www.ingramcontent.com/pod-product-compliance
Lightning Source LLC
Chambersburg PA
CBHW072045040426
42447CB00012BB/3021